POLYNESIAN STAR CATALOG:
REVISED

compiled by

Martha H. Noyes

CONTENTS

Acknowledgments   1

Preface   3

Key to References and Geogragraphical Abbreviations   7

English to Polynesian   11

Polynesian to English   79

Acknowledgments

A great many people, many long gone, provided the research that is compiled in this little book. First among them are those whose names were rarely recorded – the people of the many islands of the Pacific who shared their star knowledge.

Appreciation is also due the 19th and early 20th century researchers who collected and wrote down the information.

A special debt is due to Rubellite Kawena Johnson whose life's work has been to revive through her brilliant scholarship the knowledge of her ancestors.

I also have to thank David H. Kelley, Glen Kila, Clarence DeLude, Alika Poe Silva, Mahealani Keale, Tom Lenchanko, and Gary David Thompson.

Dedication:

To the children of Kamaile Academy.

Preface

This catalog is the work of many, many people from many places and times. Its purpose is to gather in one place as many of the known names and identities of Polynesian, particularly Hawaiian, celestial objects as can be found. It is hoped that this catalog will benefit others who would like to learn more about the ways in which Polynesians understood the sky.

That Polynesians knew the sky well is certain, as this catalog testifies. Underlying and coincident with that knowledge is an entire body of interrelated understandings of the natural world, including the very nature of knowledge and the many ways of teaching and learning.

I've made no comments, provided none of my own ideas or thoughts about the many meanings and implications of the star names. This work – the star catalog – is intended to be a tool for others to use for whatever their purposes may be and whoever they may be – scholars, cultural practitioners, students, anyone interested in Polynesian sky knowledge.

And it belongs, first and foremost, to Polynesians past and present.

The rows of stars of Kane,
The stars in the firmament,
The stars that have been fastened up,
Fast, fast, on the surface of the heaven of Kane,
And the wandering stars,
The tabued stars of Kane,
The moving stars of Kane;
Innumerable are the stars;
The large stars,
The little stars,
The red stars of Kane. O infinite space!
The great Moon of Kane,
The great Sun of Kane,
Moving, floating,
Set moving about in the great space of Kane.
The great Earth of Kane,
The Earth Kapakapaua of Kane,
The Earth that Kane set in motion,
Moving are the stars, moving is the moon,
Moving is the great Earth of Kane.

from Abraham Fornander, An Account of the Polynesian Race: Its Origin and Migrations and the Ancient History of the Hawaiian People to the Times of Kamehameha I, Volume I, London, Trubnerand Co., 1878, p. 73

Key to References

B1   Best, Elsdon, The Astronomical Knowledge of the Maori, Dominion Museum, Wellington, New Zealand 1922
http://www.nzetc.org/tm/scholarly/tei-BesAstro.html

B2   Best, Elsdon, The Maori Division of Time, R. E. Owen, Wellington, New Zealand, 1959
http://www.nzetc.org/tm/scholarly/tei-BesTime.html

B3   Best, Elsdon, Maori Star Names, Journal of the Polynesian Society, Volume 19, No. 2, 1910

B4   Best, Elsdon, Maori Religion and Mythology, Part One, A.R. Shearer, Wellington, New Zealand 1976

B5   Best, Elsdon, Maori Religion and Mythology, Part Two, A.R. Shearer, Wellington, New Zealand 1982

B6   Best, Elsdon, Maori Personifications. Anthropogeny, Solar Myths and Phallic Symbolism: as Exemplified in the Demiurgic Concepts of Tane and Tiki, Journal of the Polynesian Society, Vo. 32, No. 126, 1923

Be   Beckwith, Martha, Hawaiian Mythology, University of Hawaii Press, Honolulu, 1970

C   Collocott, E.E.V., Tongan Calendar and Astronomy, Occassional Papers of the Bernice Pauahi Bishop Museum of Polynesian ethnology and natural history, Bishop Museum Press, Honolulu 1922

Ca   Cartwright, Bruce, The legend of Hawaii-Loa, Journal of the Polynesian Society 38, 1929

Ch   Christian, F.W., Notes from the Caroline Islands, Journal of the Polynesian Society, Volume 6, No. 4, 1897

Co   Cowan, James, The Maori Yesterday and Today, Whitcomb and Tombs, 1930

Cr   Cruchet, Louis, Le Ciel en Polynesie: Essai d'ethnoastronomie en Polynesie orientale, L'Harmattan, Paris, France, 2005

E   Emory, Kenneth P., Kapingamarangi: Social and Religious Life of a Polynesian Atoll, Bernice P. Bishop Museum Bulletin 228, Honolulu, Hi 1965

EE   Edwards, Edmundo and Edwards, Alexandra, Rapanui Archaeoastronomy and Ethnoastronomy, Flag #83 Expedition Report, February-June 2010, Pacific Islands Research and Education Fund, Friday Harbor, Washington, http://www.pacificislandsresearchinstitute.org/Flag_83_Report.pdf

F1   Fornander, Abraham, An Account of the Polynesian Race: Its Origins and Migrations, V. I, Trubner and Co., London, 1878 http://www.archive.org/stream/anaccountpolyne05stokgoog#page/n9/mode/1up

F2   Fornander, Abraham, An Account of the Polynesian Race; Its Origins and Migrations, v. III, Trubner and Co., London, 1885 http://www.archive.org/stream/accountofpolynes03forn#page/n15/mode/2up

G   Grimble, Sir Arthur, Gilbertese Astronomy and Astronomical Observances, in Journal of the Polynesian Society, Volume 40, No. 160, p 197-224

Gi   Gill, William Wyatt, Myths and Songs from the South Pacific, Henry S. King and Co., London, 1876 http://www.masseiana.org/gill.htm

Gu   Gutmanis, June, The Hawaiian Sky: The Sun, Moon, Stars, and Other Phenomena, 1987, unpublished ms. Also titled Look to the

Heavens: Nana I Na Lani: Astrology, Sky Signs and Calendars of the Ancient Hawaiians.

H1   Henry, Teuira, Tahitian Astronomy, Journal of the Polynesian Society, Volume 16, No. 2., p 101-104

HI   Hiroa, Te Rangi (Peter S. Buck), Ethnology of Mangareva, Bernice P. Bishop Bulletin 157, Honolulu, Hi 1938

HH   Hare Hongi, Gods of Maori Worship, Journal of the Polynesian Society, Volume 29, No. 113, 1920

HN   Hale Naua (per Gutmanis) in Gutmanis, June, The Hawaiian Sky: The Sun, Moon, Stars, and Other Phenomena, 1987.

J1   Johnson, Rubellite Kawena, The Kumulipo Mind, A Global Heritage, Anoai Press, 2000

J2   Johnson, Rubellite Kawena and Mahelona, John Kaipo, Na Inoa Hoku, Topgallant Publishing Co., Ltd., Honolulu, 1975

JPS1   Futuna, or Horne Island and its People, Volume 1, No.1, 1892, p. 33-52

JPS2   Maori Star Names, Volume 20, No. 1, p. 10-11

JPS3   The Tahitian Version of Tafa'i, Volume 21, No. 1, p. 1-12

K   Samuel Kamakau, Instructions in Ancient Astronomy as Taught by Kaneakahoowaha, Thrum's Hawaiian Annual for 1891, Honolulu p. 142-43

K-S   Kingsley-Smith,C., Maori Star Lore, A talk to the Whakatane Astronomical Society, New Zealand, 1966
www.transitofvenus.co.nz/docs/MaoriStarLore.doc

L   Lewis, David, We, the Navigators: the Ancient Art of Landfinding in the Pacific, University of Hawaii Press, Honolulu, 1972

Le   Levard, A., translator, The Tahitian Version of Tafa'i, Journal of the Polynesian Society, Volume 21, No. 1, 1912

M1   Makemson, Maud, Hawaiian Astronomical Concepts I, American Anthropologist, Volume 40, 1938, p. 370-383

M2   Makemson, Maud, Hawaiian Astronomical Concepts II, American Anthropologist Volume 40, 1939, p. 589-595

M3   Makemson, Maud, The Morning Star Rises, Yale University Press, New Haven, 1941

PD   Paumotuan Dictionary, Journal of the Polynesian Society, Vo. 4, No. 1, 1895

PE   Pukui, Mary Kawena, and Elbert, Samuel, Hawaiian Dictionary, University of Hawaii Press, Honolulu 1986

PT Pacific Traditions website at
http://222.pacifictraditions.org/vaka/NSFNotes/html

S   Stair, John B., Rev., The Names and Movements of the Heavenly Bodies, as Looked at from a Samoan Point of View, Journal of the Polynesian Society, Volume 7, No. 1, 1898, p. 48-49

Sm   Smith, S. Percy, translator, The Lore of the Whare-Wananga: Things Celestial, New Plymouth, New Zealand, 1913, at
http://www.sacred-texts.com/pac/lww/index.htm

T   Tregear, Edward, Maori-Polynesian Comparative Dictionary, Lyon and Blair, Wellington, New Zealand, 1891

Key to Geographical Abbreviations

Ao	Aotearoa (New Zealand)
C	Cook Islands
Fi	Fiji
Fu	Futuna
H	Hawaii
Ka	Kapingamaragni
Ki	Kiribati
La	Lamotrek
Man	Mangaia
Mang	Mangareva
Mar	Marquesas
Nu	Nukuoro
P	Ponape
Rapa	Rapa Nui
Raro	Rarotonga
Sa	Samoa
SC	Santa Cruz Islands
Ta	Tahiti
Tau	Taumako
Ti	Tikopia

To   Tonga

Tu   Tuamotu

THE STAR CATALOG

English to Polynesian

Achenar	Po orongo	EE	Rapa
Acubeus	Kaulana-a-ka-la?	Gu	H
Agena	Konamaukuku	J1	
Aldebaran	Keoma	J1	H
	Aumea	J1	
	Haumea	J1	H
	Lilioma	J1	H
	Muaokeoma ?	J1	H
	Hulikahikeoma	J1	H
	Keoma-aiku	J1	H
	Oma	J1	H
	Nanahoa	J1	H
	Taumata-kuku	B1	Ao
	Te Kokota	B3	Ao
	Ana-muri	H1	Ta
	Hokuula	M2	H
	Aumea	G	

	Ana-muri	J2	
	Aumea	J2	
	Heeti	J2	
	Kao-maaiku	J2	
	Tai-rio-aitu	J2	
	Unu	J2	
	Ana-Muri	L	Ta
	Kapuahi	M3	H
	Hoku ula	Gu	H
	Kapu-ahi?	Gu	H
	Ul	Ch	La
	Makalii	Be	H
	Aumea	Gi	
	Un(u)	E	Ka
	Kete	EE	Rapa
	Aldebaran, Alpha, Delta, Theta, and Epsilon tauri		
Al Fard or Cor Hydra	Ana-heuheu-po	H1	Ta
	Ta-urua-feufeu	H1	Ta
	Ana-heuheu	J2	
	Ana-heuheu-po	J2	

	Tu-i-te-moana-urifa	J2	
	Ana-Henheu-po [sic]	L	Ta
Algol	Kane?	Gu	H
Alpha Centauri	Na-Mata-o-te-tokalua	L	C
Alpha and Beta Centauri	Ka Maile-mua and Ka Maile-hope	M3	H
	Nga Vaka	EE	Rapa
	Taura	T	Ao
Altair	Kukulukulu	J1	H
	Humuhumu	J1	H
	Nakulu	J1	H
	Liililimanu	J1	H
	Manukele	J1	H
	Kamanuhaahaa (const)	J1	H
	Kaakaa	J1	H
	Humu	J1	H
	Part of a bird const. with Procyon, Canopus, and Rigel	J1	H
	Poutu-te-rangi	K-S	Ao
	Poutu-te-rangi	B1	Ao
	Humu	K	H

	Pou-tu-te-rangi	JPS2	Ao
	Hoohumu	J2	
	Humu	J2	
	Koro-takataka	J2	
	Mailapa	J2	
	Mairapa	J2	
	Pou-tu-te-rangi	J2	
	Te-hao-o-Rua	J2	
	Takurua-whare-ana	J2	
	Takurua-pare-wai	J2	
	Tama-i-vaho	J2	
	Tolu	J2	
	Turu	J2	
	Tolu	L	C
	Humu	M3	H
	Humu	Gu	H
	Humu	PE	H
Antares	Kukulukulu	J1	H
	Polehua ?	J1	H
	Nakulu	J1	H
	Mehakuakoko ?	J1	H

Kahuaokalani	J1	H
Lehua	J1	H
Lehuaula	J1	H
Hua	J1	H
Hokuula	J1	H
Poutu-te-rangi	B1	Ao
Rehua	B1	Ao
Rerehu	B1	Ao
Ruhi (near Antares)	B1	Ao
Ruhi-te-rangi (")	B1	Ao
Whakaonge-kai (")	B1	Ao
Rehua	K-S	Ao
Ana-mua	H1	Ta
Rimwimata	G2	Ki
Atutahi-ma-Rehua	JPS2	Ao
Rerehu	JPS2	Ao
Ana-mua	J2	
Autahi-ma-Rehua	J2	
Melemele	J2	
Pou-tu-te-rangi	J2	
Pipiri	J2	

	Hai	J2	
	Rehua	J2	
	Rerehu	J2	
	Ehua	J2	
	Auhaele	J2	
	Kao	J2	
	Lehua-kona	J2	
	Welehu	J2	
	Ana-Mua	L	Ta
	Meremere	L	C
	Hoku-ula	M3	H
	Lehua-kona?	M3	H
	Hoku ula	Gu	H
	Lehua-kona?	Gu	H
	Tumur	Ch	La
	Rerehu?	T	Ao
	Meremere	E	Ka
	Rei a tanga	EE	Rapa
	Ko u tui	EE	Rapa
Aquila	Na hoku humuma	M2	H
	Paotoa	J2	

	Humu-ma	J2	
	Humu	J2	
	Humu-ma	Gu	H
	Mai-lap (Althoea and alpha Aquilae	Ch	La
	Mairapa (Altair plus beta and gamma)	E	Ka
Arcturus	Lea	J1	H
	Luulea	J1	H
	Hokulea	J1	H
	Walea	J1	H
	Lealea	J1	H
	Ruawahia	B1	H
	Ana-tahua-taata-metua-te-tapu-mavae	H1	Ta
	Hokulea	M1	H
	Romoi	J2	
	Ramoi	J2	
	Ana-tahua-taata-metua	J2	
	Hokulea	J2	
	Tavau	J2	

	Ana-Tahua-Taata-Metua- Te-Tupu-Mave	L	Ta
	Hokulea	L	H
	Tavau	L	SC
	Hoku-lea	M3	H
	Hoku lea	Gu	H
	Aramoi	Ch	La
	Hokulea	PE	H
	Romoi	E	Ka
	Ko para tahiri	EE	Rapa
Argo	Ke Alii o kona I ka lewa?	M3	H
Aries	Napaika	J2	
	Melemele	Gu	H
Arietes	Ping-en-lakh	Ch	La
Auriga	Kahinalii	J1	H
	Faa-nui	H1	Ta
	Faanui	J2	Ta
	Hoku-lei?	M3	H
	Hoku lei?	Gu	H
Baachus	Taero-aru	J2	Ta

Betelgeuse	Kaelo	J1	H
	Aua	J1	H
	Ana-varu	H1	Ta
	Taurua-nui-o-mere	H1	Ta
	Rehua	J2	
	Treka-pekau-ki-Taumako	J2	
	Ana-varu	J2	
	Ana-iva	J2	
	Taurua-nui-o-mere	J2	
	Aua	J2	
	Kaelo	J2	
	Koko	J2	
	Kahui Takurua	J2	
	Ana-Vara	L	Ta
	Trekapekau ki Taumako	L	SC
	Aua	M3	H
	Kaelo	M3	H
	Kaulua-koko	M3	H
	Melemele?	M3	H

	Aua	Gu	H
	Hoku ula	Gu	H
	Kaelo	Gu	H
	Kaulua-koko	Gu	H
	Melemele	Gu	H
	Aua	PE	H
	Kaelo	PE	H
Big Dipper	Manu	J1	H
	Manu-kaki-oa	J1	H
	Naholokauihiku	J1	H
	Na hiku	M1	H
	Na hiku	K	H
	Le Anava	S	Sa
	Manu-kaki-oa	J2	
	Na Hiku	J2	
	Na Hiku	M3	H
	Na Hiku-ka-hui-a-Makalii	M3	H
	Kiaha	M3	H
	Na-hiku-ka-huihui-a-maka-lii	Gu	H

	Ki-aha	Gu	H
	Ualego	Ch	La
	Nga toa rere	EE	Rapa
Bootes	Hoku-iwa	M3	H
	Hoku-iwa?	Gu	H
	Hoku iwa	PE	H
Cancer	Hiki-kau-lia	HN	H
Canis Major	Putahi nui o Rehua	B1	Ao
	Wai whakaata o Rehua	B1	Ao
	Taumata o Rehua	B1	Ao
	Pukawanui	B1	Ao
	Kahui takurua	B1	Ao
	Te putahi nui o Rehua	HH	Ao
	Te Wai-wakaata o Rehua	HH	Ao
	Mal	Ch	La
	Tau a aru ahu (two stars in)	EE	Rapa
Canopus	Lehuakona	J1	H
	Kona	J1	H

Hinakona	J1	H
Pakau	J1	H
Kamanuhaahaa (const)	J1	H
Mauluikonanui ?	J1	H
Auhaku	J1	H
Aotahi	B1	Ao
Atutahi	B1	Ao
Atutahi-ma-Rehua	B1	Ao
Autahi	B1	Ao
Kauanga	B1	Ao
Makahea ?	B1	
Autahi	K-S	Ao
Taurua-nui-o-te- Hiti-apatao	H1	Ta
Taurua-e-tupu-tai-nanu	H1	Ta
Autahi	JPS2	Ao
Kauanga	JPS2	Ao
Autahi	J2	
Atutahi	J2	
Atutahi-ma-Rehua	J2	

Kauanga	J2	
Makahea	J2	
Paepae-poto	J2	
Alii-o-kona-i-ka-lewa	J2	
Taurua-e-tupu-tai-naniu	J2	
Taurua-nui-o-te-hiti-apatoa	J2	
Treka-pekau-ki-Ndeni	J2	
Ti Pakau i ngeiho	J2	
Trekapekau ki Ndeni	L	SC
Ke Alii o kona i ka lewa?	M3	H
Haka-moa?	Gu	H
Hakaka-a-moa?	Gu	H
Haku-po-kano	Gu	H
Aotahi	T	Ao
Autahi	T	Ao
Aututahi	T	Ao
Kauanga	T	Ao
Tutahi	T	Ao
Ti Pakau i ngeiho	E	Ka

	Po roroa	EE	Rapa
Capella	Kahinalii	J1	H
	Tahi-arii	H1	Ta
	Hokulei	M2	H
	Matariki	J2	
	Mata-tau-inoa	J2	
	Tahiarii	J2	
	Tarang(a)	J2	
	Hoku-lei?	M3	H
	Hoku lei?	Gu	H
	Evang-el-ul	Ch	La
	Tarang(a)	E	Ka
Capella and Menkalinan	Ko toe ko peu renga	EE	Rapa
Capricornus	Rua-o-mere	H1	Ta
	Apu-o-te-rai	J2	
	Rua-o-Mere	J2	
	Kaulua	HN	H
Cassiopeia	Mulehu, Poloula, and Poloahilani as Alpha, Beta, And Gamma	M3	H

	Mulehu, Poloula, and Polo-ahi-lani	Gu	H
	Yuk-ol-ik	Ch	La
Castor	Whakaahu	B1	Ao
	Whakaahu	M1	
	Nana-mua	M3	H
	Nana-mua	Gu	H
	Hilinehu	PE	H
	Hilina ehu	PE	H
Castor and Pollux	Ka Maile-mua and Ka Maile Hope	M3	H
Centauri	Ti-humu-uri (alpha)	J2	
	Ti-humu-uri (beta)	J2	
	Ti-humu-uri (alpha)	E	Ka
	Ti-humu-te	E	Ka
	Ti-humu-mhe (alpha) E		Ka
Cetus	Na Hoku-pa (head of)	M3	H
	Hoku pa (head of)	Gu	H
	Hoku pa (head of)?	PE	H

Coalsack	Manako-uri	B1	Ao
	Patiki	B1	Ao
	Rua-patiki	B1	Ao
	Rua-o-mahu	B1	Ao
	Whai-a-titipa	B1	Ao
	Naha	B1	Ao
	Te patiki	K-S	Ao
	Sumu	JPS	Fu
	Hotu-te-ihi-rangi	J2	
	Kokiri	J2	
	Manakouri	J2	
	Naha	J2	
	Patiki	J2	
	Piawai	J2	
	Rangawhenua	J2	
	Totara	J2	
	Urua	J2	
	Pulele-hua-kawaewae	M3	H
	Te Riu o Maahu	Co	Ao

Constellation	Huhui	F2	H
Corona	Tchrou	Ch	La
Corona Australis	Te Baraitoa ?	G2	Ki
Corona Borealis	Kaua-mea?	M3	H
	Kao-maka-lii	Gu	H
	Kaua-mea	Gu	H
Corvus	Metua-ai-papa	H1	Ta
	Mee	J2	Mar
	Sor-a-bol	Ch	La
Crater	Moana-ohu-noa- ei-haa-moe-hara	H1	Ta
Cygnus	Tuula-lupe ?	M2	
Cygnus and Delphini	Ti Kumate	J2	
Delphinus	Pau-ahi	Gu	H
Delphius	Ti Kumat(e)	E	Ka
Deneb	Pirae-tea	H1	Ta
	Taurua-i-te-haapa- raa-manu	H1	Ta
	Pirae-tea	J2	
	Taurua-i-te-haaparaa-manu	J2	

	Kawai ?	E	Ka
Dubhe	Ana-tipu	H1	Ta
	Le Anava	J2	Sa
	Le Toloa	J2	Sa
	Taulua-tua-fanua	J2	
	Taulua-alofi	J2	
	Ana-tipu	J2	
Ecliptic	Ke ala a ke kuukuu	J1	H
	Whitireia	T	Ao
	Matangi-reia	Sm	Ao
	Ara-tukutuku	Sm	Ao
Equator	Houpo	J1	H
	Kapapaiakea	J1	H
	Wakea	J1	H
	Kahiki ke papa lani	M1	H
	Ke Ala-ulu a ke kuukuu	F1	H
	Ke Ala i ka piko o Wakea	F1	H
	Ke alanui a ke kuukuu	PE	H
	Alanui	PE	H

	Piko o Wakea	PE	H
Equinox	Kaitara	G2	Ki
Eridanus	Waihau	Sm	Ao
Fomalhaut	Taurua	H1	Ta
	Taurua-i-te-ia-o-te-noo	H1	Ta
	Taurua-nui-	J2	
	Taurua-i-te-ia-o-te-noo	J2	
	Hatu-tahi	J2	
	Veri koreha	EE	Rapa
Gemini	Poulua	J1	H
	Kaulua	J1	H
	Muaokahana ?	J1	H
	Hanakaulua	J1	H
	Mahanakaulua	J1	H
	Na Mahoe	J1	H
	Mahoe mua (Castor)	J1	H
	Mahoe hope (Pollux)	J1	H
	Pipili (or Scorpius)	J1	H
	Lalohana (w. of meridian)	J1	H

	Mahapili	J1	H
	Hanalaanui and Hanalaaiki	J1	H
	Faa-tapotupotu	H1	Ta
	Nanahope and Nanamua	M2	H
	Makalii	K	H
(eastern twin)	Filo-momea	JPS1	Fu
(western twin)	Tapuke-tea	JPS1	Fu
	Tautama	JPS1	Fu
	Ngana	J2	
	Ngana-te-unu-mea	J2	
	Pipiri-ma	J2	
	Ehua	J2	
	Whaka-ahu	J2	
	Ka-mahana	J2	
	Na Mahoe	J2	
	Filo-momea	J2	Fu
	Tau-tama	J2	Fu
	Taulua	J2	SC
	Luatangata	C	Sa

	Kamahana	M3	H
	Mahana	M3	H
	Na Hoku Mahana	M3	H
	Mahau	M3	H
	Na Mahoe	M3	H
	Kaelo	Gu	H
	Ka-mahana	Gu	H
	Mahana	Gu	H
	Mahoe	Gu	H
	Makalii	Gu	H
	Na-lalani-o-pililua	Gu	H
	Na-mahoe	Gu	H
	Mongoi-sap	Ch	La
	Mahana	T	Ao
	Luatagata	T	Sa
	Te hau vaero	EE	Rapa
Gemini and Sirius	Kaulualena	J1	H
Gomeisa and Procyon	Tauru nukunuku	EE	Rapa
Grus	Ti Matira	J2	

	Ti Pa (Alpha)	J2	
	Te Matira	E	Ka
	Ti Pa (alpha)	E	Ka
Halley's Comet	Awa-nui-a-rangi	HH	Ao
Hama	Kaa-lolo	Gu	H
Hercules	Maui (together with Sagittarius and Ophiucus)	J1	H
	Maui Loa	J1	H
	Maui Kane	J1	H
Hyades	Te kokota	K-S	Ao
	Mata	B1	Ao
	Mata-kaheru	B1	Ao
	Kanukuokauahi	M2	H
	Ka-nuku-o-kapuahi	J2	
	Matakaheru	J2	
	Ka-nuku-o-kapuahi	M3	H
	Ka-nuku-o-kapuahi	Gu	H
	Nga rau hiva	EE	Rapa
Hydra	Tu-ite-moana-urifa	H1	Ta
Clear sky under Hydra	Moana-aere	H1	Ta

Juno	Kaa-lalo	HN	H
Jupiter	Iwa	J1	H
	Hua	J1	H
	Iao	J1	H
	Leleiao (morning)	J1	H
	Poiao (evening)	J1	H
	Kahuaokalani	J1	H
	Kaawela	J1	H
	Kahua	J1	H
	Huanuiekalalailaika (morn.)	J1	H
	Kalolomaiao	J1	H
	Kalalamaiao	J1	H
	Wailea	J1	H
	Hine-i-tiweka	B1	Ao
	Parearau	B1	Ao
	Kopu-nui	B1	Ao
	Taurua-nui	H1	Ta
	Taurua-o-rai-taetaea- o-hawaii-i-te-tua	H1	Ta
	Taurua-e-hiti-i-ara-o-te-		

anuanua	H1	Ta
Parearau	K-S	Ao
Iao	M2	H
Ikaika	M2	H
Kaawela	K	H
Fetu-aasoa	JPS1	Fu
Fetu-ea	JPS1	Fu
Tupua-lengase	S	Sa
Tiriao	JPS2	Ao
Aohoku	J2	
Fetu-Aasoa	J2	
Fetu-ea	J2	
Hine-i-te-weka	J2	
Hoomanalo	J2	
Iao	J2	
Ikaika	J2	
Ikiiki	J2	
Kaawela?	J2	
Ehua	J2	

Tupua-le-ngase	J2	
Takurua-rau	J2	
Tari-ao	J2	
Taurua-e-hiti-i-ara-o-te-anuanua	J2	
Taurua-o-rai-taetaea-o-Havaii-i-te-fua	J2	
Iao	F1	H
Hoomanalonalo	F1	H
Ikaika	F1	H
Ikaika	M3	H
Ikiiki	M3	H
Kaawela	M3	H
Kawela	M3	H
Hoomanalonalo	M3	H
Iao	M3	H
Ao-hoku?	M3	H
Au-huku?	M3	H
Au-haku?	M3	H
Hua	M3	H

	Ao-hoku	Gu	H
	Iao	Gu	H
	Ikaika	Gu	H
	Ikiiki	Gu	H
	Kaawela	Gu	H
	Kawela	Gu	H
	Manalo	Gu	H
	Mananalo	Gu	H
	Hoomanalo	Gu	H
	Aohoku	PE	H
	Iao (morning)	PE	H
	Iao (morning)	T	
	Rehua ?	T	Ao
	Fetiapoipoi	T	Ta
	Hoku hikina ku o na aina (as morning star)	Ca	H
Leo	Kakau	B1	Ao
	Na Hoku pa?	M3	H
	Hoku pa?	Gu	H
	Hoku pa?	PE	H

Leo and Hydra	Te-rai-tu-roroa	H1	Ta
Leshaa (in Scorpius)	Potiki	J2	Raro
Libra	Welo	HN	H
Little Dipper	Manu	J1	H
	Manu-kaki-oa	J1	H
	Na Hiku	J2	
	Hiku-lii	Gu	H
Lyra	Aliikaea	J1	H
	Kehooea	J1	H
	Kehooea	J2	
	Keoe	M3	H
	Keoea	M3	H
	Kaoea	Gu	H
	Keoe	Gu	H
	Kaoea (or Keoe) and the stars Kukui-o-kona-mukuku, Ka-uhi-o-maohai, and Kau-lua-koakoa	Gu	H
	Kautoki	E	Ka
	Me-mua	E	Ka
Magellanic clouds	Mahukona	J1	H

(one or both)

Kona	J1	H
Hinakona	J1	H
Pulelehu	J1	H
Manako-tea	B1	Ao
Nga Patari	B1	Ao
Nga Pataritari-hau	B1	Ao
Nga Patari-kai-hau	B1	Ao
Nonoko-tea	B1	Ao
Nonoko-uri	B1	Ao
Nga Patari-hau	B1	Ao
Purangi	B1	Ao
Tiripua	B1	Ao
Tiritiripua	B1	Ao
Whakaruru-hau	B1	Ao
Kokouri	B1	Ao
Kokotea	B1	Ao
Ao-uri	B1	Ao
Ao-tea	B1	Ao
Tuputuputu	K-S	Ao

	Te-waka-ruru	KS	Ao
	Nga mau	G	Ki
	Ao-tea	J2	
	Kokiri	J2	
	Mahu-	J2	
	Patari	J2	
	Te-Mango-roa	J2	
	Ripua	J2	
	Pulelehua-	J2	
(nebula west of)	Maafu-lele	JPS1	Fu
(nebula east of)	Maafu-toka	JPS1	Fu
	Takuura	JPS2	Ao
	Na mahu	L	C
	Onga Maafu	L	To
	Rua Mafu	L	C
	Pulelehua	Gu	H
	Katipar	Ch	P
	Nga mau	Gi	
Magellanic Cloud Large	Kokirikiri	B1	Ao

	Patari-rangi	B1	Ao
	Rangi-matanuku	B1	Ao
	Tioreore	B1	Ao
	Maafu-toka	C	To
	Luamafu	L	SC
	Pulele-hua-kea	M3	H
Magellanic Cloud Small	Patari-Kaihau	B1	Ao
	Tikatakata	B1	Ao
	Maafu-lele	C	To
	Pulele-hua-uli	M3	H
Magellanic Cloud Lower	Mahu-raro	H1	Ta
Magellanic Cloud Upper	Mahu-nia	H1	Ta
Mars	Mata whero	B1	Ao
	Rangiwhenua	K-S	Ao
	Maunu-ura	H1	Ta
	Hokuula	M2	H
	Holoholopinau	M2	H
	Hokuula	K	H
	Mata-memea	S	Sa

Te-Hau-o-Rua	J2	
Horo-pukupuku	J2	
Au-kele-nui-a-iku	J2	
Holoholo-pinaau	J2	
Parearau	J2	
Mata-memea	J2	
Maunu Ura	J2	
Holoholopinau	F1	H
Matamemea	C	To
Hoku-ula	M3	H
Holoholo-pinaau	M3	H
Au-kele-ni[sic]-a-iku	Gu	H
Au-kele	Gu	H
Hoku ula	Gu	H
Kawela	HN	H
Kaawela	HN	H
Holoholopina'au	PE	H
Fetiaura	T	Ta
Matamea	EE	Rapa

Menkalinan and Capella	Ko toe ko peu renga	EE	Rapa
Mercury	Kaawela	J1	H
	Whiro	B1	Ao
	Takero	K-S	Ao
	Ukahialii	M2	H
	Ukali	K	H
	Le-Soa-o-Tapuitea	J2	
	Le-Taelo	J2	
	Kaawela	F1	H
	Hoku-ula	F1	H
	Ukali	M3	H
	Ukaliialii	M3	H
	Kaawela	M3	H
	Hoku ula	Gu	H
	Holoholo-pi-naau	HN	H
	Ukali	Gu	H
	Ukali-alii	Gu	H
	Tariao	Co	Ao
Meridian	Moa	J1	H

Milky Way	Ia	J1	H
	Aikanaka	J1	H
	Moo	J1	H
	Pae	J1	H
	Paeloahiki	J1	H
	Mokukapewa	J1	H
	Mokukaia	J1	H
	Kupolohaihai	J1	H
	Polohaihai	J1	H
	Haihai	J1	H
	Alii	J1	H
	Olii	J1	H
	Moolio	J1	H
	Muaokahanuu ?	J1	H
	Muaokahai ?	J1	H
	Meheia	J1	H
	Kauluokaoka	J1	H
	Mohai	J1	H
	Niu-loa-hiki	J1	H

Tuahiwi-nui-o-rangi	B1	Ao
Ika a Maui	B1	Ao
Ika-matua a Tangaroa	B1	Ao
Ikaroa	B1	Ao
Ika-whenua-o-te-rangi	B1	Ao
Mangaroa	B1	Ao
Mokoroa-i-ata	B1	Ao
Paeroa o Whanui	B1	Ao
Tuahiwi o Rangi-nui	B1	Ao
Whiti-kaupeka	B1	Ao
Te kupenga a Taramainuku	B1	Ao
Te ika-o-te-Rangi	K-S	Ao
Mangaroa	K-S	Ao
Vai-ora-a-Tane	H1	Ta
Faarava-i-te-rai (the long clear space in the MW, the shark in his pool)	H1	Ta
Lalani	M2	H
Kuamoo	M2	H
Kaniva	JPS	Fu

Mango-roa	JPS2	Ao
Arokeva	J2	
Kaniva	J2	
Le Ao-lele	J2	
Na Kiore	J2	
Te-ika-kau-ki-rangi	J2	
Te-Mango-roa	J2	
Moko-roa-i-ata	J2	
Patiki	J2	
Tarava	J2	
Vai-ora-a-Tane	J2	
Tangaroa	J2	
Hoku-noho-aupuni	J2	
Kau	J2	
Pae-loa-hiki	J2	
Kuamoo	J2	
Kaniva	C	To
Aniva	C	Sa
Ia	M3	H

	Kau	M3	H
	Lalani	M3	H
	Pae-loa-hiki	M3	H
	Hii-o-ka-lani	Gu	H
	Hoku noho aupuni	Gu	H
	Ia	Gu	H
	Ia-lele-iakea	Gu	H
	Kau	Gu	H
	Kua-moo	Gu	H
	Lalani	Gu	H
	Pae-loa-hiki	Gu	H
	Hoku noho aupuni	PE	H
	Ika-roa	T	Ao
	Ika-o-te-rangi	T	Ao
	Mangoroa	T	Ao
	Magaroa-i-ata	Hi	Mang
	Te ngoe	EE	Rapa
Mira	Kane?	Gu	H
Navigators' star course or Path(way)	Alanui o na hoku hookele	PE	H

	Hoku ai aina	PE	H
Ophiucus with Hercules and Sagittarius	Maui	J1	H
	Maui Loa	J1	H
	Maui Kane	J1	H
Orbit	ala poai	PE	H
Orion	Amo	J1	H
	Heamo	J1	H
	Heamokau	J1	H
	Keaomele (at equator)	J1	H
	Kakau	B1	Ao
	Kakau a Maui	B1	Ao
	Pewa a Tautoru	B1	Ao
	Te-uru-meremere	H1	Ta
	Hau-o-rua	K-S	Ao
	Ke Kaka (part of Orion)	K-S	Ao
	Na Kao	K	H
	Alotolu	J2	
	Tolu	J2	

	Tautoru	J2	
	Amonga	J2	Sa
	Taurua-o-mere-ma-tutahi	J2	
	Maiaku	J2	
	Mutu	J2	
	Melemele	J2	
	Tuke-a-Maui	J2	
	Tuitui-hohe	J2	
	Ti-Waka-to(ko)toru	J2	
	Ti Tui	J2	
	Turuturu-ti-harau	J2	
	Alotolu	C	To
	Arotoru	L	Ti
	Oliel	Ch	La
	Turuturu-ti-rarau (alpha, Kappa, beta, and gamma)	E	Ka
	E tui	EE	Rapa
Orion's Belt	Tau Toro	K-S	Ao
	Melemele	J1	H
	Nakao	J1	H

Maui-a-ka-malo	J1	H
Welo	J1	H
Maui's skylifting pole	J1	H
Mere	H	Ta
Taurua-o-mere-ma-tu-tahi	H	Ta
Hao-o-rua (near Orion's Belt	B1	Ao
Tautoro	B1	Ao
Tata o Tautoro	B1	Ao
Tira o Puanga	B1	Ao
Tuke o Tautoro	B1	Ao
Nga Whata	B1	Ao
Tuke a Maui	B1	Ao
Tautoru	M1	
Na Kao	M2	H
Tolu	JPS1	Fu
Amonga	S	Sa
Hui-tarawa	F2	Ta
Te-tolunga-Maui	L	C
Na Kao (and Sword)	M3	H

	Maia-ku	M3	H
	Na Kao	Gu	H
	Maia-ku	Gu	H
	Melemele	Gu	H
	Huitarava	T	Ta
	Ti Waka-tokotoru	E	Ka
	Te Tui (sword in)	E	Ka
	Tautoru	HI	Mang
	Tautoru	EE	Rapa
	Takelo	PT	Tau
	Nga Tira a Puaka	Co	Ao
Paris (asteroid)	Hina-ma-lailena	HN	H
	Hina-o-na-lailena	HN	H
Pegasus	Aliilaa	J1	H
	Laa	J1	H
	Polaa	J1	H
	Laka	J1	H
	An eel	J1	H
	Gapi-lah	Ch	La

Perseus	Kanakaopeopenui	J1	H
	Faa-iti	H1	Ta
	Fsaa-iti	J2	Ta
Phaet	Ana-iwa	H1	Ta
	Ana-iwa	J2	Ta
Phact	Ana-iwa	L	Ta
Pisces	Ik	Ch	La
Piscis Australis	Taki-piti-tolu	J1	
	Atu-tahi	H1	Ta
	Atutahi	J2	Ta
(two stars near)	Fetau-ngapepe	JPS1	Fu
	Ngi-tau	Ch	La
Piscis	Uliuli	HN	H
Pleiades	Liiokioki	J1	H
	Alii	J1	H
	Olii	J1	H
	Kekelii	J1	H
	Makalii	J1	H
	Aliikilo	J1	H

Konamaukuku ?	J1	H
Na Huihui	J1	H
Huihuikau o Makalii	J1	H
Matariki	B1	Ao
Huihui o Matariki	B1	Ao
Ao-Kai	B1	Ao
Tupua-nuku (one of)	B1	Ao
Tupua-rangi (")	B1	Ao
Waiti (")	B1	Ao
Waipuna-a-rangi (")	B1	Ao
Ururangi (")	B1	Ao
Hoko-kumara	B1	Ao
Matariki	K-S	Ao
Tipua-nuku (one of)	K-S	Ao
Tipua-rangi (")	K-S	Ao
Waiti (")	K-S	Ao
Waiata (")	K-S	Ao
Waipuna-o-rangi	K-S	Ao
Uru-rangi	K-S	Ao

Mata-rii	H1	Ao
Na Huihui	M2	H
Matariki	G	
Huihui	K	H
Nei Auti	G2	Ki
Mata-liki	JPS1	Fu
Lii	S	Sa
Mata-riki	JPS2	Ao
Matariki	J2	
Le tuingalama	J2	
Tau-ono	J2	
Wai-puna-o-rangi	J2	
Waita	J2	
Waiti	J2	
Ke-whetu-nawenewene	J2	
Huihui	J2	
Kupuku	J2	
Makarii	F1	H
Mataliki	C	To

Fetu Matoro	L	SC
Na Huihui	M3	H
Na Huihui-a-Makalii	M3	H
Ka Huihui-pa-ipu-a-Makalii	M3	H
Makalii	M3	H
Huihui	Gu	H
Ka-huihui-pa-ipu-Makalii	Gu	H
Ku-puku	Gu	G
Kupuku	Gu	H
Makeriker	Ch	P
Magarigar	Ch	La
Kalalaniamakalii	PE	H
Na koko a Makalii	Be	H
Na huihui a Makalii	Be	H
Matariki	Gi	
Matariki	T	Ao
Matalii	T	Sa
Makalii	T	H
Mataliki	T	To

	Mataiki	T	Mar
	Matariki	T	Man
	Matariki	T	Mang
	Matariki	E	Ka
	Matariki-tinitini	HI	Mang
	Matariki	EE	Rapa
	Hetu Mdavo	PT	Tau
Pleiades with Perseus	Kalalani	J1	H
Polaris	Kakio	J1	H
	Kiopaa	J1	H
	Kioio	J1	H
	Hokupaa	J1	H
	Kio	J1	H
	Ana-nia	H1	Ta
	Kiopaa	M2	H
	Hoku Paa	K	H
	Ana-nia	J2	
	Hokupaa	J2	
	Kiopaa	J2	

	Kumau	J2	
	Noho-loa	J2	
	Ana-Nia	L	Ta
	Hoku-paa	M3	H
	Kiopaa	M3	H
	Kumau	M3	H
	Noho-loa	M3	H
	Hoku paa	Gu	H
	Kio-paa	Gu	H
	Kukui	Gu	H
	Kumau	Gu	H
	Maka-holo-waa	Gu	H
	Uioliuil-al-evang	Ch	La
	Hoku paa	PE	H
Pollux	Nana-hope	M3	H
	Nana-hope	Gu	H
Post, pillar, brace, prop	Koo		
	Pou		
	Loaa		

	Kulu		
	Kapoukiaokalani		
	Kookookalani		
	Kakukuinanahua		
	Kia		
Procyon	Pakau	J1	H
	Liililimanu	J1	H
	Manukele	J1	H
	Puangahori	B1	Ao
	Ana-tahua-vahine-o-te-manava	H1	Ta
	Puanga hori	K-S	Ao
	Vena	G	Ki
	Puanga-hori	JPS2	Ao
	Taulua (Pileni)	J2	
	Ana-tahua-vahine-o-toa-te-manava	J2	
	Puanga-hori	J2	
	Ti Pakau i ngake	J2	
	Ana-Tahua-Vahine-O-Toa Te-Manava	L	Ta

	Puangahori	T	Ao
	Ti Pakau i ngake	E	Ka
Procyon as part of a bird (manu) constellation with Canopus, Rigel, and Altair	Kamanuhaahaa	J1	H
Procyon and Gomeisa	Tauru nukunuku	EE	Rapa
Regulus	Ikiiki	J1	H
	Kauopae	J1	H
	Palolo-muli	JPS	Fu
	Palolo-muli	J2	Fu
	Ililigak	Ch	La
Rigel	Puanga	K-S	Ao
	Kauopae	M2	H
	Puanakau	J1	H
	Poaka	B1	Ao
	Puaka	B1	Ao
	Puanga	B1	Ao
	Puangarua	B1	Ao
	Pua-tawhiki-a-tautoru	B1	Ao

	Te Taubuki	G2	Ki
	Puanga	JPS2	Ao
	Manu	J2	
	Puanga	J2	
	Manu	L	Ti
	Puana-kau	M3	H
	Pua-na-kau	Gu	H
	Puaka	T	Ao
	Puanga	T	Ao
	Tau ahu	EE	Rapa
Rigel in bird constellation with Procyon, Canopus, and Altair	Kamanuhaahaa	J1	H
Rigel and Castor	Nga Tokorua a Taingarue	B1	Ao
Sagittarius	Maitiki	J2	Nu
	Kaaona	HN	H
Sagittarius (Southern Crown in)	Tanuma	JPS1	Fu
Sagittarius with Hercules and Ophiucus	Maui	J1	H
	Maui Loa	J1	H

	Maui Kane	J1	H
Saturn	Makulukulu	J1	H
	Nakulu	J1	H
	Hine-i-tiweka	B1	Ao
	Parearau	B1	Ao
	Fetu-tea	H1	Ta
	Holoholopinau	K	H
	Fetu-aasoa	JPS1	Fu
	Fetu-ea	JPS1	Fu
	Fetu-tea	J2	Ta
	Makulukulu	J2	H
	Naholoholo	M3	H
	Makulu	M3	H
	Makalu	M3	H
Scorpius	Makau	J1	H
	Pipili (or Gemini)	J1	H
	Manaia-ka-lani	J1	H
	Pekehawani (a star in)	B1	Ao

Rehua	B1	Ao
Waka o Mairerangi (hook)	B1	Ao
Waka o Tamarereti (tail)	B1	Ao
Whare-o-te-whiu	B1	Ao
Te-waka-o-Tama (tail)	K-S	Ao
Te-waka-o-Taina (tail)	K-S	Ao
Ka-makau-nui-o-Maui	J2	
Te-matau-o-Maui	J2	
Metarik	J2	
Nga Piri	J2	
Pipiri-ma	J2	
Potiki (Shaula)	J2	
Tara-korekore	J2	
Te-waka-o-Tama-rereti	J2	
Te-waka-o-Tamamairerangi	J2	
Ikiiki	HN	H
Met-a-ryo	Ch	La

Scorpius – black nebula
nearby together with

Pisces australis	Te tao o Maui	J1	
Seres (asteroid)	Ka-maile-hope	HN	H
Shaula	Mohalu	J1	H
Sigma and Tau Scorpii	Auhaele and Paikauhale	M3	H
Sigma	Au-haele	Gu	H
Sirius	Loaa ke Kane	J1	H
	Haaa	J1	H
	Hokukelewaa	J1	H
	Kapoulena	J1	H
	Oa	J1	H
	Lono	J1	H
	A	J1	H
	Lena	J1	H
	Aaa	J1	H
	Aamoa (at the meridian)	J1	H
	Kaloloaa (at the zenith)	J1	H
	Lenawale	J1	H
	Hikikauelia	J1	H
	Hulumalailena	J1	H

Hikawaolena	J1	H
Lonomai	J1	H
Lonoaakaikai	J1	H
Kahailono	J1	H
Takurua	K-S	Ao
Takurua	B1	Ao
Taurua-nui-i-te-amoaha	H1	Ta
Taurua-fau-papa	H1	Ta
Turua-e-hiti-i-te-tara-te-feiai	H1	Ta
Hookelewaa	M2	H
Ka hoku hookelewaa	K	H
Palolo-mua	JPS	Fu
Telengese	S	Sa
Takurua	JPS2	Ao
Aa	J2	
A-iki-kau-e-Lono	J2	
Mere	J2	
Lena	J2	
Rehua	J2	

Takurua	J2	
Taurua-fau-papa	J2	
Taurua-e-hiti-i-te-tara-te-fei	J2	
Taurua-i-te-amo-aha	J2	
Sino	J2	
Tele-ngese	J2	
Te Kokota	J2	
Palolo-mua	J2	
Etu-tu-taka-ao	J2	
Manu	J2	
Aa	M3	H
Hiki-kauelia	M3	H
Hiki Kauilia	M3	H
Hiki-kau-lono-meha	M3	H
Hoku-hookelewaa	M3	H
Kau-ano-meha	M3	H
Kaulua	M3	H
Kaulua-ihai-mohai	M3	H
Kaulua-lena	M3	H

Kauopae	M3	H
Aa	Gu	H
Hiki-kau-lia	Gu	H
Hoku-hookele-waa	Gu	H
Ka-ua-meha?	Gu	H
Kau-ano-meha?	Gu	H
Ka-ulu-i-kua?	Gu	H
Kaulua	Gu	H
Kaulua-lena	Gu	H
Kauopae	Gu	H
Lena	Gu	H
Lono	Gu	H
Te Ura-te-turu	Le	Ta
Kolong-al-mal	Ch	La
Aikikauelono	PE	H
Hikikauelono	PE	H
Hikikauelia	PE	H
Hikikaulia	PE	H
Hokuhookelewaa	PE	H

	Hokukauopae	PE	H
	Hoku opae	PE	H
	Hikikaulonomeha	PE	H
	Mere	Gi	
	Takurua	T	Ao
	Meremere	T	Man
	Takarua	T	Ao
	Manu	E	Ka
	Te pou o te rangi	EE	Rapa
	Sino	PT	Tau
Solstice	Koi	J1	H
	Koiele	J1	H
	Kamoleokahunua (solstice point)	J1	H
	Mole (northwest solstice limit)	J1	H
	toki	G2	Ki
	Buatarawa (of the north)	G2	Ki
	Bike ni Kanenei-ang (south)	G2	Ki
	Rua maoro	F1	Ta

	Rua poto	F1	Ta
	Takanga a te ra	B1	Ao
	Hikumutu (June)	B1	Ao
	Maruaroa	B2	Ao
	Haronga (summer)	B6	Ao
	Ruaroa (southern tropic, summer solstice)	PD	Pau
	Ruapoto (northern tropic, winter solstice)	PD	Pau
	Marua-roa-o-te-Takurua (south of equator, winter)	Sm	Ao
	Marua-roa-o-te-Orongonui (south of equator, summer)	Sm	Ao
Southern Cross	Kea	J1	H
	Pea	J1	H
	Wene	J1	H
	Newa	J1	H
	Humuhumu	J1	H
	Lelekeamo	J1	H
	Newaiku	J1	H
	Makeamo	J1	H

Newaku	J1	H
Aliinewa	J1	H
Loiloikopea	J1	H
Kopea	J1	H
Moa	J1	H
Peapea	J1	H
Kapeakau	J1	H
Kamakanewe	J1	H
Oili	J1	H
Oililolo	J1	H
Makeaupea	J1	H
Kahui o Mahutonga	B1	Ao
Kahui-ruamahu	B1	Ao
Te Putea iti a reti	B1	Ao
Taki o Autahi	B1	Ao
Te Whai a Titipa ?	B1	Ao
Tau-ha	H1	Ta
Mahutonga	K-S	Ao
Hoku-kea	M1	H

Hakamoa	M2	H
Newe	K	H
Kama	G2	Ki
Moa	JPS1	Fu
Kauvakorna	J2	Fi
Moa	J2	Fu
Ko-peka	J2	Tu
Napahata	J2	
Rakau Tapu	J2	Ti
Rua Tangata	J2	Ti
Toloa	J2	To
Te-Mango-Roa-hei-kapu	J2	
Te-Mango-roa-hei-puku	J2	
Te-uru-o-te-rangi	J2	
Tauha	J2	
Mahu-tonga	J2	
Marere-o-Tonga	J2	
Taki-o-Autahi	J2	
Tatauro	J2	

Hanai-a-ka-malama	J2	
Hoku-kea	J2	
Sumu	J2	
Toloa	C	To
Rakau Tapu	L	Ti
Rakau Tangata	L	Ti
Hanaia-kamalama	M3	H
Hoku-kea	M3	H
Ka-pea	M3	H
Newa	M3	H
Newe	M3	H
Newenewe	M3	H
Hana-a-ka-malama [sic]	Gu	H
Hoku kea	Gu	H
Ka-peaa	Gu	H
Kohema-lama-lama	Gu	H
Newe	Gu	H
Hoku-kea-o-ka-mole-honua	M3	H
Mel	Ch	P

	Uiliuil-al-eaur	Ch	La
	Pup	Ch	La
	Hokukea	PE	H
	Mata te tautoro (3 stars in)	EE	Rapa
Spica	Maliu	J1	H
	Whiki-kaupeka	B1	Ao
	Mariao ?	B1	Ao
	Mariua	B1	Ao
	Ana-roto	H1	Ta
	Peke-hawani	JPS2	Ao
	Ana-roto	J2	
	Mariua	J2	
	Peke-hawanui	J2	
	Ruhi	J2	
	Hikinalia	J2	
	Harapori	J2	
	Ana-Roto	L	Ta
	Hiki-ana-lia	Gu	H
	Hiki au-moana	Gu	H

	Hiki au	Gu	H
	Harapori	E	Ka
	Ko te mata nui	EE	Rapa
Spider (and web)	Punanana	J1	H
	Punanailanaia	J1	H
Spider	Kuukuu	J1	H
Sun	Loiloila	J1	H
	Ka onohi o ka la	J1	H
	Tama nui te ra	B1	Ao
	Wanaku (rising)	J1	H
	Ra tuoi	B4	Ao
	Ra kura	B5	Ao
	Hana	PD	Pau
Taurus	Hinaiaeleele	HN	H
Tau scorpii	Pai-ka-hale	Gu	H
Tropic of Cancer	Loiokane	J1	H
	Ke ala polohiwa a Kane	J1	H
	Kahiki kapua holani ke kuina	M1	H
	Ke alanui polohiwa a Kane	K	H

	Ke Ala-nui polohiwa a Kane	F1	H
Tropic of Capricorn	Loiokanaloa	J1	H
	Ke ala polohiwa a Kanaloa	J1	H
	Kahiki ke papa nuu	M1	H
	Ke alanui polohiwa a Kanaloa	K	H
	Ke Ala-nui polohiwa a Kanaloa	F1	H
Vega	Keoea	J1	H
	Kehooea	J1	H
	Whanui	B1	Ao
	Whakakorongata ?	B1	Ao
	Whanui	K-S	Ao
	Keoe ?	K	Ao
	Whanui	JPS2	Ao
	Meremere	JPS2	Ao
	Whanui	J2	
	Meremere	J2	
	Kautoki	J2	
	Me-mua	J2	

	Meisik	J2	
	Kaoea	Gu	H
	Keoe	Gu	H
	Meal (with alpha Lyrae)	Ch	La
	Whanui	Be	Ao
	Whanui	T	Ao
	Veri hariu	EE	Rapa
Venus	Pulukea	J1	H
	Kea	J1	H
	Loa	J1	H
	Hokuloa	J1	H
	Kaawela	J1	H
	Mananalo (disappearing)	J1	H
	Kopu (eve)	B1	Ao
	Meremere	B1	Ao
	Meremere-tu-ahiahi (eve)	B1	Ao
	Rangi-ahiahi (eve)	B1	Ao
	Rere-ahiahi (eve)	B1	Ao
	Tawera (morn)	B1	Ao

Tawera (morn)	K-S	Ao
Meremere	K-S	Ao
Tuurua	H1	Ta
Taurua-e-hiti-i-matavai	H1	Ta
Taurua-i-te-pati-fetia	H1	Ta
Hokuloa	M2	H
Hoku-alii-wahine	M2	H
Kaawela	M2	H
Ka-eleele o ka wanaoa	M2	H
Ka hoku komohana	M2	H
Kahela	M2	H
Hokuloa	K	H
Tamatanui	G	
Fetu-ao (morning)	JPS1	Fu
Malama-kainga	JPS1	Fu
Tapuitea	S	Sa
Kopu-parapara	JPS2	Ao
Kopu (morning)	JPS2	Ao
Tawera	JPS2	Ao

Meremere	JPS2	Ao
Akatauira	J2	
Fetu-Ao	J2	
Kopu	J2	
Rere-ahiahi	J2	
Tapukitea	J2	
Te-mata-nui-o-Tane	J2	
Tawera	J2	
Meremere	J2	
Taurua-	J2	
Hoku-alii-wahine	J2	
Hoku-Ao	J2	
Hoku-kau-ahiahi	J2	
Hoku-komohana	J2	
Hoku-loa	J2	
Holo-i-Kahiki	J2	
Kaawela	J2	
Kaeleele-o-ka-wanaao	J2	
Mulehu	J2	

Na-holoholo	J2	
Manapu-upuute-ahiahi	J2	
Hetu-nui	J2	
Pukute(a)	J2	
Noholoholo	F1	H
Hoku-loa	M3	H
Hoku-alii	M3	H
Noholoholo	M3	H
Hoku-komohana (evening)	M3	H
Hoku-alii	Gu	H
Hoku-ao	Gu	H
Hoku-komohana	Gu	H
Hoku-loa	Gu	H
Mulehu	Gu	H
Holo-i-kahiki	Gu	H
Kaawela	Gu	H
Kawela	Gu	H
Manalo	Gu	H
Mananalo	Gu	H

Hoomanalo	Gu	H
Oa-urua-horo-ahiahi	Le	Ta
Ta Ura-i-tia-hotu	Le	Ta
Hoku ao	PE	H
Kaeleeleokawanaao	PE	H
Tamatanui, morning	Gi	
Takurua-rau, evening	Gi	
Taurua	T	Ta
Tawera, morning	T	Ao
Kaawela, evening	T	H
Fetiapoipoi	T	Ta
Ava-te-rehurehu	HI	Mang
Hetuu ahiahi, evening	EE	Rapa
Hetuu popohanga, morn	EE	Rapa
Hoku hikina ku o na aina (as morning star)	Ca	H
Puaroa	Sm	Ao
Taurua-tuira-horo-ahiata (morning)	JPS3	Ta
Oa-urua-horo-ahiahi (evening)	JPS3	Ta

Vero (in Orion's Belt)	Weloka	J1	H
Vesta (asteroid)	Ka-maile-mua	HN	H
Virgo	Nana	HN	H
Zenith	Hui	J1	H
	Nuu	J1	H
	Halawai	J1	H
	Muanuunuu	J1	H
	Loiloikapu	J1	H
	Loilalolo	J1	H
	Piopio	J1	H
	Kealanuu	J1	H
	Lolo	J1	H
	Akilolo	J1	H
	Huina	J1	H
	Pionuu	J1	H
	Nuunuu	J1	H
	Lilinuunuu	J1	H
	Aliikilokau	J1	H
	Muaokahanuu	J1	H

Loiloipololo	J1	H
Kulukau	J1	H
Ololonuu	J1	H
Nalaunuu	J1	H
Kupukuanuu	J1	H
Luanuu	J1	H
Luanuukahiko (old zenith)	J1	H
Piowai	J1	H
Kalolomauna	J1	H
Kalolomoana	J1	H
Kalolopiko	J1	H
Keleikanuulani (navigate zenith)	J1	H
Nuualani	J1	H
Kalolo	J1	H
Oililolo	J1	H
Pioalani	J1	H
Hookui	PE	H
Lolopua	PE	H
Kahiki-kapu-i-Holani-ke-	PE	H

kuina

Hikialoalo	PE	H
Wekea	PE	H

Polynesian to English

A	Sirius
Aa	Sirius
Aaa	Sirius
Aamoa	Sirius (at the meridian)
Aikanaka	Milky Way
A-iki-kau-e-Lono	Sirius
Akilolo	Zenith
Alanui o na hokuhookele	navigators' star path or course
Ala-poai	orbit (circular path)
Alii	Pleiades; Milky Way
Aliikaea	Lyra
Aliikilo	Pleiades
Aliikilokau	Zenith
Aliilaa	Pegasus
Aliinewa	Southern Cross
Alii-o-kona-i-ka-lewa	Canopus
Alotolu	part of Orion
Amo	Orion

Amonga	Orion
Ana-heuheu-po	Al Fard or Cor Hydra
Ana-Henheu-Po [typo?]	Alphard
Ana-iwa	Phaet; Phact
Ana-mua	Antares
Ana-muri	Aldebaran
Ana-nia	Polaris
Ana-roto	Spica
Ana-tahua-taata- metua-te-tapu-mavae	Arcturus
Ana-tahua-vahine-o-te-manava	Procyon
Ana-tipu	Dubhe
Ana-Vara	Betelgeuse
Ana-waru	Betelgeuse
Aniva	Milky Way
Ao-hoku	Jupiter
Ao-huku?	Jupiter
Ao-haku?	Jupiter
Ao-kai	Pleiades
Aotahi	Canopus

Ao-tea	Magellanic Cloud(s)
Ao-uri	Magellanic Cloud(s)
Ara-tukutuku	Ecliptic
Aramoi	Arcturus
Arotoru	Orion
Atutahi	Canopus
Atu-tahi	Canopus
Atutahi-ma-Rehua	Canopus
Aua	Betelgeuse
Auhaku	Canopus
Au-haele	Sima
Aukele-nui-a-iku	Mars?; Aldebaran
Au-kele	Mars
Aumea	Aldebaran
Autahi	Canopus
Ava-i-te-rehurehu	Venus
Awa-nui-a-rangi	Halley's Comet
Bike ni Kanenei-ang	south solstice
Buatarawa	north solstice

Evang-el-ul	Capella
E tui	Orion
Faa-iti	Perseus
Faa-nui	Auriga
Faarava-i-te-rai	the long clear space in the Milky Way (the shark in his pool)
Faa-tapotupotu	Gemini
Fetau-ngapepe	two stars near Pisces australis
Fetiapoipoi	Venus; Jupiter
Fetiaura	Mars
Fetu-aasoa	Saturn; Jupiter
Fetu-ea	Saturn; Jupiter
Fetu Matoro	Pleiades
Fetu-tea	Saturn
Filo-momea	eastern Gemini twin
Gapi-lah	Pegasus
Haaa	Sirius
Haihai	Milky Way
Hakamoa	Southern Cross

Halawai	Zenith
Hana	Sun
Hanai-a-ka-malama	Southern Cross
Hanaia-kamalama	Southern Cross
Hanakaulua	Gemini
Hanalaaiki	one of the Gemini twins
Hanalaanui	one of the Gemini twins
Hao-o-rua	near Orion's Belt
Harapori	Spica
Haronga	summer (Aotearoa) solstice
Heamo	Orion
Heamokau	Orion
Hetu Mdavo	Pleiades
Hetuu ahiahi	Venus, evening
Hetuu popohanga	Venus, morning
Hii-o-ka-lani	Milky Way
Hikawaolena	Sirius
Hikialoalo	Zenith
Hikianalia	"computed as Spica"

Hiki-au-moana	Spica
Hikikauelia	Sirius; Cancer (HN)
Hiki-kau-e-lono	Sirius
Hiki-kau-e-lono-meha	Sirius
Hiki Kauilia	Sirius
Hikikaulia	Sirius
Hiku-lii	Little Dipper
Hilina ehu	Castor
Hilinehu	Castor
Hinaiaeleele	Taurus (HN)
Hina-ma-lailena	Paris (asteroid; HN)
Hina-o-na-lailena	Paris (asteroid: HN)
Hinakona	Canopus; Magellanic Cloud(s)
Hine-i-tiweka	Saturn; Jupiter
Hoko-kumara	Pleiades
Hoku-alii	Venus
Hoku-ao	Venus (morning)
Hoku-alii-wahine	Venus
Hoku hikina ku o na aina	Venus (morning); Jupiter (morning)

Hoku-hookelewaa	Sirius
Hoku-iwa	Bootes?
Hoku-kau-ahiahi	Venus (evening)
Hokukauopae	Sirius
Hoku-kea	Southern Cross
Hokukelewaa	Sirius
Hoku-komohana	Venus (morning)
Hoku-komohana	Venus (evening)
Hokulea	Arcturus
Hokulei	Cappela
Hoku-lei	Auriga
Hokuloa	Venus
Hokunohoaupuni	Milky Way
Hoku Pa	Leo; head of Cetus
Hokupaa	Polaris
Hokuula	Mars; Aldebaran; Antares
Holoholopinau	Mars; Saturn
Holoholo-pi-naau	Mercury (HN)
Holo-i-kahiki	Venus

Hoohumu	Altair
Hookelewaa	Sirius
Hookui	zenith
Hoomanalonalo	Jupiter; Venus
Houpo	Equator
Hua	Antares; Jupiter
Huanuiekalaailaika	Jupiter
Huhui	constellation
Hui	Zenith
Huihui o Matariki	Pleiades
Huihui	Pleiades
Huihuikau o Makaliii	Pleiades
Huihui-koko-a-makalii-kau-i-luna	Pleiades
Huihui-pa-ipu-a-makalii	Pleiades
Huina	Zenith
Hui-tarawa	Orion's Belt
Huitarava	Orion's Belt
Hulikahikaoma	Aldebaran
Hulumalailena	Sirius

Humu	Altair; dark patch near left hand end of Southern Cross
Humuhumu	Altair; Southern Cross
Ia	Milky Way
Ia-lele-iakea	Milky Way
Iao	Jupiter; Jupiter as morning star
Ik	Pisces
Ika a Maui	Milky Way
Ikaika	Jupiter
Ika-matua a Tangaroa	Milky Way
Ika-o-te-rangi	Milky Way
Ikaroa	Milky Way
Ika-whenua-o-te-rangi	Milky Way
Ikiiki	Regulus; Jupiter; Scorpio (HN)
Ililigak	Regulus
Iwa	Jupiter; Equator
Kaa-lalo	Juno (HN)
Kaa-lolo	Hama?
Kaakaa	Altair

Kawela	Jupiter; Mercury; Venus
Kaawela	Jupiter; Mercury; Venus; Venus, evening
Ka-eleele o ka wanaoa	Venus
Kaelo	Betelgeuse; Gemini
Kahailono	Lono
Kahela	Venus
Kahiki kapua holani ke kuina	Tropic of Cancer; zenith
Kahiki ke papa lani	Equator
Kahiki ke papa nuu	Tropic of Capricorn
Kahinalii	Capella; Auriga
Kahua	Jupiter
Kahuaokalani	Jupiter; Antares
Kahui o Mahutonga	Southern Cross
Kahui takurua	Canis Major
Kahui-ruamahu	Southern Cross
Kaitara	Equinox
Kakau a Maui	Orion
Kakau	Leo; Orion
Kakio	Polaris

Kakukuinanahua	Post, pillar
Kalalamaiao	Jupiter
Kalalani	Pleiades with Persus
Kalalani a Makalii	Pleiades
Kalaniopuu	same as Kawela (Jupiter; Mercury; Venus)
Kalolo	Zenith
Kaloloaa	Sirius at zenith
Kalolomaiao	Jupiter (at zenith?)
Kalolomauna	Zenith
Kalolomoana	Zenith
Kalolopiko	Zenith
Kama	Southern Cross
Kamahana	Gemini
Kamailehope	one of the Gemini twins; either alpha or beta Centauri; Seres (asteroid, HN)
Kamailemua	same as above; Vesta (asteroid, HN)
Kamakanewe	Southern Cross
Kamanuhaahaa	bird constellation with Procyon, Altair, Rigel, and Canopus
Kamoleokahunua	Solstice point

Kanakaopepenui	Perseus
Kane	Sun; Mira?; Algol?
Kaniva	Milky Way
Ka-nuku-o-kapuahi	Hyades
Kanukuokauahi	Hyades
Kao	Antares; Orion's Belt and sword
Kaomaaiku	Aldebaran
Kao-maka-lii	Corona Borealis?
Ka onohi o ka la	Sun
Kapapaiakea	Equator
Kapea	Southern Cross
Kapeaa	Southern Cross
Kapeakau	Southern Cross
Kapoukiaokalani	Polaris
Kapoulena	Sirius
Kapu-ahi	Aldebaran
Katipar	Magellanic Cloud(s)
Kau	Milky Way
Kaua-mea	Corona Borealis?

Kauanga	Canopus
Kau-ano-meha	Sirius
Kaulana-a-ka-la	Acubeus?
Kaulu	Southern Cross
Kaulua	Gemini; Sirius
Kaulua-ahai-mohai	Sirius?
Kaulua-koko	Betelgeuse
Kaulualena	Gemini and Sirius; Sirius
Kauluokaoka	Milky Way
Kauopae	Regulus; Rigel; Sirius
Kautoki	Vega plus epsilon, zeta, and delta Lyrae
Kawai	Deneb ?
Ke ala a ke kuukuu	Ecliptic
Ke ala polohiwa a Kanaloa	Tropic of Capricorn
Ke ala polohiwa a Kane	Tropic of Cancer
Ke alanui polohiwa a Kanaloa	Tropic of Capricorn
Ke alanui polohiwa a Kane	Tropic of Cancer
Ke ala-ula o ke kuukuu	Equator
Kea	Southern Cross; Venus

Ke-alii-o-kona-i-ka-lewa	Canopus
Kealanuu	Zenith
Keaomele	Orion (at equator)
Kehooea	Vega; Lyra
Kekelii	Pleiades
Keleikanuulani	navigate zenith
Kelewaa	Sirius
Keoe	Vega?
Keoea	Vega
Keoma	Aldebaran
Keoma-aiku	Aldebaran
Kete	Aldebaran and Delta, Theta, and Epsilon Taurii
Kia	Polaris
Kiaha	Big Dipper
Kio	Polaris
Kioio	Polaris
Kiopaa	Polaris
Kohema-lama-lama	Southern Cross

Koi	Solstice
Koiele	Solstice
Kokirikiri	Large Magellanic Cloud
Koko	Betelgeuse
Kokotea	Magellanic Cloud(s)
Kokouri	Magellanic Cloud(s)
Kolong-al-mal	Sirius
Kona	Canopus; Magellanic Cloud(s)
Konamaukuku	Pleiades; Agena
Koo	Post, pillar
Kookookalani	Post, pillar
Ko para tahiri	Arcturus
Kopea	Southern Cross
Kopu	Venus (evening); Venus (morning)
Kopu-nui	Jupiter
Kopu-parapara	Venus
Ko pu tui	Antares
Ko te mata pu nui	Spica
Ko toe ko peu renga	Menkalinan and Capella

Kuamoo	Milky Way
Kukui	Polaris
Kukulukulu	Altair; Antares
Kulu	Post, pillar
Kulukau	Zenith
Kumau	Polaris
Kupolohaihai	Milky Way
Kupuku	Pleiades
Kupukuanuu	Zenith
Kuukuu	Spider (ecliptic)
Laa	Pegasus
Laka	Pegasus
Lalani	Milky Way
Lalohana	Gemini (W. of meridian)
Lea	Arcturus
Lealea	Arcturus
Le Anava	Big Dipper
Lehua	Antares
Lehuakona	Canopus; Antares

Lehuaula	Antares
Lele-aka	Milky Way
Leleiao	Jupiter (morning)
Lelekeamo	Southern Cross
Lena	Sirius
Lenawale	Sirius
Lii	Pleiades
Liililimanu	Altair; Procyon
Liiokioki	Pleiades
Lilinuu	Zenith
Lilioma	Aldebaran
Loa	Venus
Loaa	Post, pillar
Loaa ke Kane	Sirius
Loilalolo	Zenith
Loiloikapu	Zenith
Loiloikopea	Southern Cross
Loiloila	Sun
Loiloipololo	Zenith

Loiokanaloa	Tropic of Capricorn
Loiokane	Tropic of Cancer
Lolo	Zenith
Lolopua	Zenith
Lono	Sirius
Lonoaakaikai	Sirius
Lonomai	Sirius
Lono-meha	Sirius
Luanuu	Zenith
Luanuukahiko	Old Zenith
Luatangata	Castor and Pollux
Luatagata	Castor and Pollux
Luulea	Arcturus
Maafu-lele	nebula W. of Magellanic Cloud(s)
Maafu-toka	nebula E. of Magellanic Cloud(s)
Magarigar	Pleaides
Magaroa-i-ata	Milky Way
Mahanakaulua	Gemini
Mahana	Gemini

Mahapili	Gemini
Mahau	Gemini
Mahoe	Gemini
Mahoe hope	Pollux
Mahoe mua	Castor
Mahukona	Magellanic Cloud(s)
Mahu-nia	Upper Magellanic Cloud
Mahu-raro	Lower Magellanic Cloud
Mahutonga	Southern Cross
Maiaku	Orion's Belt
Mailap	Althoea and alpha Aquilae
Mairapa	Altair plus beta and gamma Aquilae
Makahea	Canopus
Maka-holo-waa	Polaris?
Makalii	Pleiades; Gemini; Aldebaran
Makalu	Saturn
Makariker	Pleiades
Makau	Scorpius
Makeamo	Southern Cross

Makeaupea	Southern Cross
Makulukulu	Saturn
Mal	Canis Major
Malama-kainga	Venus
Maliu	Spica
Manai-a-kalana	Scorpius
Manaia-ka-lani	Scorpius
Manako-tea	Magellanic Cloud(s)
Manako-uri	Magellanic Cloud(s)
Mananalo	Venus (disappearing)
Mangoroa	Milky Way
Manu	Big Dipper; Little Dipper; Rigel; Sirius
Manu-kaki-oa	Big Dipper; Little Dipper
Manukele	Procyon
Mariao	Spica?
Mariua	Spica
Maruaroa	Solstice
Marua-roa-o-te-Orononui	Summer solstice, south of equator
Marua-roa-o-te-Takurua	Winter solstice, south of equator

Mataiki	Pleiades
Mata-kaheru	Hyades
Matalii	Pleiades
Mata-liki	Pleiades
Mataliki	Pleiades
Matamea	Mars
Mata-memea	Mars
Matamemea	Mars
Matangi-reia	Ecliptic
Mata-rii	Pleiades
Matariki	Pleiades
Mata-riki	Pleiades
Matariki-tinitini	Pleiades
Mata te tautoru	3 stars in Southern Cross
Mata whero	Mars
Maui	constellation made up of parts of Sagittarius, Ophiucus, and Hercules
Maui Kane	constellation made up of parts of Sagittarius, Ophiucus, and Hercules
Maui Loa	constellation made up of parts of Sagittarius, Ophiucus, and Hercules

Maui-a-ka-malo	Orion's Belt
Mauluikonanui	Canopus
Maunu-uru	Mars
Meal	Vega and alpha Lyrae
Mehakuakoko	Antares?
Mehaia	Milky Way
Mel	Southern Cross
Melemele	Orion's Belt; Antares; Betelgeuse
Me-mua	Vega plus epsilon, zeta, and delta Lyrae
Mere	Orion's Belt; Sirius
Meremere	Vega; Venus; Sirius; Antares
Meremere-tu-ahiahi	Venus (evening)
Met-a-ryo	Scorpius
Metua-ai-papa	Corvus
Moa	Meridian; Southern Cross
Moana-aere	clear sky under Hydra
Moana-ohu-noa- ei-haa-moe-hara	Crater
Mohai	Milky Way

Mohalu	Shaula
Mokoroa-i-ata	Milky Way
Mokukaia	Milky Way
Mokukapewa	Milky Way
Mole	northwest solstice point
Mongoi-sap	Gemini
Moo	Milky Way
Moolio	Milky Way
Muanuunuu	Zenith
Muaokahai	Milky Way?
Muaokahana	Gemini?
Muaokahanuu	Milky Way?; zenith
Muaokeoma	Aldebaran
Mulehu	Venus?; a star in Cassiopeia?
Na hiku	Big Dipper
Na hoku humuma	Aquila
Na Hoku pa	head of Cetus?
Na-holoholo	Venus
Na huihui	Pleiades

Na-huihui-o-Makalii	Pleiades
Na kao	Orion; Orion's Belt
Na-koko-a-Makalii	Pleiades
Na-lalani-o-pililua	Gemini
Naha	Coalsack
Na Hiku-ka-huihui-a-Makalii	Big Dipper
Naholokauihiku	Big Dipper
Na Huihui-a-Makalii	Pleiades
Nakao	Orion's Belt
Nakulu	Saturn; Altair; Antares
Nalaunuu	Zenith
Na Mahoe	Gemini
Na Mahu	Magellanic Clouds
Na Mata-o-te-tokalua	Alpha Centauri
Nana	Virgo (HN)
Nanahoa	Aldebaran
Nanahope and Nanamua	Gemini
Nana-hope	Pollux
Nana-mua	Castor

Nei Auti	Pleiades
Newa	Southern Cross
Na-wahine-o-makalii	Pleiades
Newa	Southern Cross
Newaiku	Southern Cross
Newe	Southern Cross
Newenewe	Southern Cross
Nga mau	Magellanic Cloud(s)
Nga Patari	Magellanic Cloud(s)
Nga Patari-hau	Magellanic Cloud(s)
Nga Patari-kai-hau	Magellanic Cloud(s)
Nga rau hiva	Hyades
Nga Tira a Puaka	Orion's Belt
Nga toa rere	Big Dipper
Nga Tokurua a Taingarue	Magellanic Cloud(s)
Nga vaka	Alpha and Beta Centauri
Nga Whata	Orion's Belt
Ngi-tau	Piscis Australis
Niu-loa-hiki	Milky Way

Noho-loa	Polaris
Nonoko-tea	Magellanic Cloud(s)
Nonoko-uri	Magellanic Cloud(s)
Nuu	Zenith
Nuualani	Zenith
Nuunuu	Zenith
Oa	Sirius
Oa-urua-horo-ahiahi	Venus (evening)
Oili	Southern Cross
Oililolo	Southern Cross
Oliel	Orion
Olii	Milky Way; Pleaides
Ololonuu	Zenith
Oma	Aldebaran
Onga Maafu	Magellanic Clouds
Pae	Milky Way
Paeloahiki	Milky Way
Paeroa o Whanui	Milky Way
Pai-ka-hale	Tau scorpii

Pakau	Procyon; Canopus
Palolo-mua	Sirius
Palolo-muli	Regulus
Parearau	Saturn; Jupiter
Patari-Kaihau	Small Magellanic Cloud
Patari-rangi	Large Magellanic Cloud
Patiki	Coalsack
Pea	Southern Cross
Peapea	Southern Cross
Pekehawani	a star in Scorpius
Peke-hawani	Spica
Pewa a Tautoru	Orion
Ping-en-lakh	Arietes
Pioalani	Zenith
Pionuu	Zenith
Piopio	Zenith
Piowai	Zenith
Pipili	Gemini; Scorpius
Pirae-tea	Deneb

Poaka	Rigel
Poiao	Jupiter (evening)
Polaa	Pegasus
Polehua	Antares
Po orongo	Achenar
Po roroa	Canopus
Poutu-te-rangi	Aldebaran; Antares
Puaka	Rigel
Puana	Rigel
Puanakau	Rigel
Puanga hori	Procyon
Puanga	Rigel
Puangahori	Procyon
Puangarua	Rigel
Puaroa	Venus
Pua-tawhiki-a-tautoru	Rigel
Pukawanui	Canis major
Pulelehu	Magellanic Cloud(s)
Pulelehua	Magellanic Clouds

Pulelehua-kawaewae	Coalsack
Pulelehua-kea	Greater Magellanic Cloud
Pulelehua-uli	Lesser Magellanic Cloud
Pulukea	Venus
Punanailanaia	Spider's nest/web
Punanana	Spider's nest/web
Pup	Southern Cross
Purangi	Magellanic Cloud(s)
Putahi nui o Rehua	Canis major
Rakau Tapu	Southern Cross
Rangi-ahiahi	Venus (evening)
Rangi-matanuku	Large Magellanic Cloud
Rangiwhenua	Mars
Rehua	Antares; Scorpius; Jupiter
Rei a tanga	Antares
Rere-ahiahi	Venus
Rerehu	Antares
Rimwimata	Antares
Romoi	Arcturus

Rua Mafu	Magellanic Clouds
Rua-maoro	December solstice
Rua-o-mahu	Coalsack
Rua-o-mere	Capricornus
Rua-patiki	Coalsack
Rua-poto	June solstice (Aotearoa); northern tropic
Ruaroa	summer solstice (Aotearoa); southern tropic
Rua Tangata	Southern Cross
Ruawahia	Arcturus
Ruhi	a star near Antares
Ruhi-te-rangi	a star near Antares
Sino	Sirius
Sor-a-bol	Corvus
Sumu	Coalsack
Tahi-arii	Capella
Tainui (canoe)	from Pleiades through Orion's Belt, with Southern Cross as anchor
Takelo	Orion's Belt
Takero	Mercury
Taki o Autahi	Southern Cross

Taki-piti-tolu	Pisces Australis
Takurua	Sirius
Tama nui te ra	Sun
Tamatanui	Venus
Tanuma	Southern Crown in Sagittarius
Tapuitea	Venus
Tapuke-tea	Gemini's western twin
Tarang(a)	Capella
Tata o Tautoro	Orion's Belt
Tau a aru ahu	two stars in Canis Major
Tau ahu	Rigel
Tau-ha	Southern Cross
Taumata-kuku	Aldebaran
Taumata o Rehua	Canis major
Taura	alpha and beta Centauri
Taura nukunuku	Procyon and Gomeisa
Taurua	Fomalhaut; Venus
Taurua-e-hiti-ara-o-te-anuanua	Jupiter
Taurua-e-hiti-i-matavai	Venus

Taurua-e-tupu-tai-nanu	Canopus
Taurua-fau-papa	Sirius
Ta-urua-feufeu	Al fard or Cor hydra
Taurua-horo-a-ahiata	Venus (morning)
Taurua-i-te-haapa-raa-manu	Deneb
Taurua-i-te-ia-o-te-noo	Fomalhaut
Taurua-i-te-pati-fetia	Venus
Taurua-nui	Jupiter
Taurua-nui-i-te-amoaha	Sirius
Taurua-nui-o-mere	Betelgeuse
Taurua-o-mere-ma-tu-tahi	Orion's Belt
Taurua-o-rai-taetaea-o-hawaii-i-te-tua	Jupiter
Tautama	Gemini
Tautoro	Orion's Belt
Tautoru	Orion's Belt
Tavau	Arcturus
Tawera	Venus; Venus (morning)
Tchrou	Corona

Te Kaka	Orion (part of)
Te Ra o Tainui	Hyades (sail of Tainui)
Te Baraitoa	Corona Australis?
Te hau vero	Castor and Pollux
Te ika-o-te-rangi	Milky Way
Te kokota	Hyades; Aldebaran
Te kupenga a Taramainuku	Milky Way
Telengese	Sirius
Te ngoe	Milky Way
Te patiki	Coalsack
Te Putea iti a reti	Southern Cross
Te tao o Maui	Black nebula near Scorpius together with Pisces Australis
Te Taubuki	Rigel
Te-rai-tu-roroa	Leo and Hydra
Te Rua o Maahu	Coalsack
Te Riu o Maahu	Coalsack
Te Tolunga-Maui	Orion's Belt
Te Ura-i-tia-hotu	Venus (morning)

Te Ura-te-uru	Sirius
Te-uru-meremere	Orion
Te-waka-o-Taina	Tail of Scorpius
Te-waka-o-Tama	Tail of Scorpius
Te waka o Tamareti	Tail of Scorpius
Te whai a titipa	Southern Cross
Ti Humu-mhe	Alpha Centaurus
Ti Humu-te	Beta Centaurus
Ti Humu-uri	Alpha Centaurus
Tikatakata	Small Magellanic Cloud
Ti Kumat(e)	Delphius
Ti Matira	Grus
Tioreore	Large Magellanic Cloud
Ti Pa	Alpha in Grus
Ti Pakau i ngeiho	Canopus
Ti Pakau i ngake	Procyon
Tipua-nuku	one of the Pleiades
Tipua-rangi	one of the Pleiades
Tira o Puanga	Orion's Belt

Tiriao	Jupiter; Mercury
Tiripua	Magellanic Cloud(s)
Tiritiripua	Magellanic Cloud(s)
Ti Tui	sword in Orion's Belt
Ti Waka-tokotoru	Orion's Belt
Toki	Sun's limit; solstice
Toloa	Southern Cross
Tolu	Orion's Belt; Altair
Trekapekau ki Ndeni	Canopus
Trekapekau ki Taumako	Betelgeuse
Tuahiwi-nui-o-rangi	Milky Way
Tuahiwi o Rangi-nui	Milky Way
Tu-ite-moana-urifa	Hydra
Tuke a Maui	Orion's Belt
Tuke o Tautoro	Orion's Belt
Tumur	Antares
Tupua-lengase	Jupiter
Tupua-nuku	one of the Pleiades
Tupua-rangi	one of the Pleiades

Tuputuputu	Magellanic Cloud(s)
Turua-e-hiti-i-te-tara-te-feiai	Sirius
Turuturu-ti-harau	alpha, kappa, beta, and gamma in Orion
Tutahi	Canopus
Tuula-lupe	Cygnus?
Tuurua	Venus
Ualego	Big Dipper
Uiliuil-al-eaur	Southern Cross
Uiliuil-al-evang	Polaris
Ukahialii	Mercury
Ukali	Mercury
Ul	Aldebaran
Uliuli	Pisces (HN)
Un(u)	Aldebaran
Ururangi	one of the Pleiades
Uru-rangi	one of the Pleiades
Vai-ora-a-Tane	Milky Way
Vena	Procyon
Veri hariu	Vega

Veri koreha	Fomalhaut
Waiata	one of the Pleiades
Waihau	Eridanus
Wailea	Jupiter
Waipuna-a-rangi	one of the Pleiades
Waipuna-o-rangi	one of the Pleiades
Waiti	one of the Pleiades
Wai whakaata o Rehua	Canis major
Waka o Mairerangi	hook of Scorpius
Waka o Tamarereti	tail of Scorpius
Wakea	equator
Walea	Arcturus
Wanaku	Sun (rising)
Wekea	Zenith
Welo	Orion's Belt; Libra (HN)
Weloka	Vero in Orion's Belt
Wene	Southern Cross
Whai-a-titipa	Coalsack
Whakaahu	Castor

Whakakorongata	Vega?
Whakaonge-kai	a star near Antares?
Whakaruru-hau	Magellanic Cloud(s)
Whanui	Vega
Whare-o-te-whiu	Scorpius
Whiki-kaupeka	Spica
Whiro	Mercury
Whiti-kaupeka	Milky Way
Whitireia	Ecliptic
Yuk-ol-ik	Cassiopoeia

The Origin of Light

Those members of the primal offspring who remained in this upper world were sore oppressed by the gloomy light that here obtained. It was Tane who introduced the clear, bright light we know, he who set on high the whanau marama, the light-giving family, the Children of Light, the heavenly bodies. These Shining Ones were arranged on the breast of Rangi, the Sky Parent, by Tane-te-waiora, and to each member was assigned the path he must traverse. So the sun, moon, and stars appeared, and so the maramatanga taiahoaho (clear enduring light) entered the world.

From Elsdon Best, The Maori As He Was: A Brief Account of Life as it Was in Pre-European Days, Dominion Museum, Wellington, New Zealand, 1934, p. 36.